FEATHERSTONE
Bloomsbury Publishing Plc
50 Bedford Square, London, WC1B 3DP, UK
29 Earlsfort Terrace, Dublin 2, Ireland

BLOOMSBURY, FEATHERSTONE and the Feather logo are trademarks of Bloomsbury Publishing Plc

First published in Great Britain 2021 by Bloomsbury Publishing Plc
Text copyright © Penny Tassoni, 2021
Illustrations copyright © Mel Four, 2021

Penny Tassoni and Mel Four have asserted their rights under the Copyright, Designs and Patents Act,
1988, to be identified as Author and Illustrator of this work

A catalogue record for this book is available from the British Library

ISBN: HB: 978-1-4729-7812-7; ePDF: 978-1-4729-7813-4; ePub: 978-1-4729-7811-0

2 4 6 8 10 9 7 5 3 1

Printed and bound in China by Leo Paper Products, Heshan, Guangdong

To find out more about our authors and books visit www.bloomsbury.com and sign up for our newsletters

Time to Go to Bed

Penny Tassoni

Illustrated by Mel Four

FEATHERSTONE
LONDON   OXFORD   NEW YORK   NEW DELHI   SYDNEY

Everyone needs to sleep...

And sometimes in the day.

Where do you sleep?

Sleep helps you to stay healthy and happy...

so you can enjoy your day.

There are times when you may need to sleep more.

When you are poorly.

And when things are busy and new.

Here are some signs that it's time to sleep.

When you feel tired.

Or you get really SILLY!

To get ready
for sleep you can...

Have a bath or shower.

Put comfortable clothes on.

What do you wear to go to bed?

You can
share
a story.

And have a cuddle.

But sleep
can't come...

when you bounce
about and play.

Or when you sing or shout.

So lights out, settle down.

Try closing your eyes.

When you wake up...

You'll be happy and ready to play.

Notes for parents and carers

Sleep is vital for children's growth and development. It helps children to learn, but also regulate their emotions. This is why tantrums and outbursts of frustration are more likely to happen as children get tired. It can be tricky to get children to sleep, though. Children need to be sufficiently relaxed. They also need to be able to self-settle. This is the ability to fall asleep without any props such as a dummy, or being rocked. You can help your child by making sure they do not become overtired and also by developing a strong sleep routine.

Sleep is so important in your child's development, that if you are having problems, it is always worth talking to your health visitor or looking at the NHS website. Here are a few helpful tips:

- Get your child outdoors as much as possible. Physical activity helps sleep.

- Make sure your child has spent enough time winding down before a nap or bedtime - at least 20 minutes.

- Avoid screen time in the hour before sleep.

- Keep light low in the run up to bedtime.

- Remove toys or things that might be a distraction.

- Outline the process of bedtime, e.g. we will have two stories, then a cuddle and then lights out.

- Talk calmly and slowly to create a bedtime mood.

- Cuddle and stroke your child as this can help them to relax.

- Share a story or two while they are in bed.

- If you need to alter bed times, do so gradually by five or ten minutes each day.

Finally, think about the amount of attention that you give your child in the day. Some children prolong bedtime in order to gain their parents' attention. Making time for play and conversations with your child during the day can help them stick to a bedtime routine.